D0828786

LONDON

See the Sights and tick them off

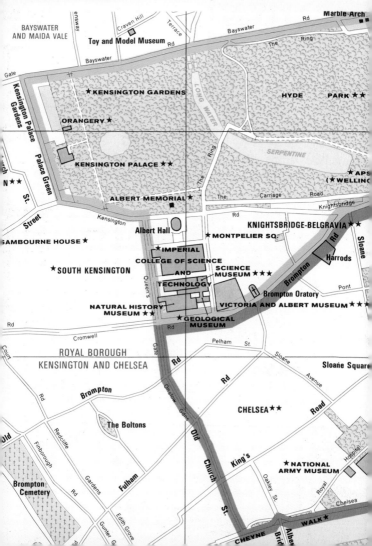

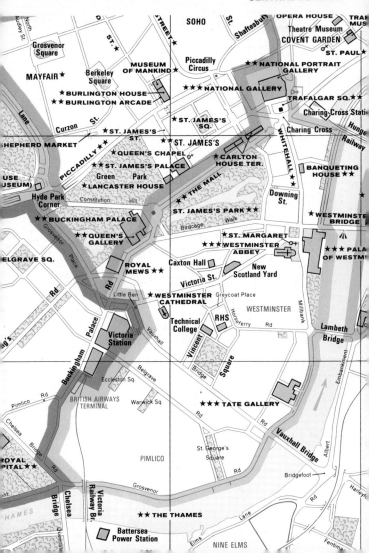

CENTRAL LONDON

SOHO

OPERA HOUSE

Theatre Museum
COVENT GARDEN

ST. PAUL

Grosvenor
Square

Piccadilly
Circus

★★ NATIONAL PORTRAIT
GALLERY

MAYFAIR ★

Berkeley
Square

MUSEUM
OF MANKIND ★

★★★ NATIONAL GALLERY

TRAFALGAR SQ. ★★

★ BURLINGTON HOUSE
★★ BURLINGTON ARCADE

★ ST. JAMES'S
SQ.

Charing Cross Station

Charing Cross

Curzon

St.

Hunge

★ ST. JAMES'S
ST.

HEPHERD MARKET

PICCADILLY ★★

★★ ST. JAMES'S

WHITEHALL

Railway

★ Queen's Chapel

★★ CARLTON
HOUSE TER.

BANQUETING
HOUSE ★★

USE
USEUM)

★★ ST. JAMES'S PALACE

Green   Park

★ LANCASTER HOUSE

★★ THE MALL

Downing
St.

Hyde Park
Corner

Constitution   Hill

★ WESTMINSTER
BRIDGE

★★ BUCKINGHAM PALACE

St. JAMES'S PARK ★★

Birdcage   Walk

★★ QUEEN'S
GALLERY

ELGRAVE SQ.

ROYAL
MEWS ★★

Caxton Hall

★ ST. MARGARET

★★★ WESTMINSTER
ABBEY

★★★ PALA
OF WESTM

New
Scotland Yard

Victoria St.

★ WESTMINSTER
CATHEDRAL

Greycoat Place

WESTMINSTER

Little Ben

Technical
College

RHS

Horseferry   Rd

Lambeth
Bridge

Victoria
Station

Vauxhall

Vincent

Square

Millbank

Eccleston Sq.

Belgrave

Bridge

BRITISH AIRWAYS
TERMINAL

Warwick Sq.

★★★ TATE GALLERY

Pimlico   Rd

Chelsea

Rd

Vauxhall Bridge

ROYAL
PITAL ★★

Chelsea

Rd

PIMLICO

St. George's
Square

Rd

Bridgefoot

Harley

Grosvenor

Rd

THAMES

Victoria
Railway Br.

★★ THE THAMES

Lane

Elms

Fentima

Battersea
Power Station

NINE ELMS

CENTRAL LONDON

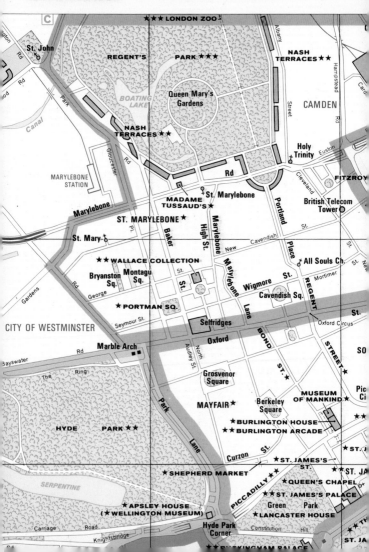

★★★ LONDON ZOO

REGENT'S **PARK** ★★★

NASH TERRACES ★★

CAMDEN

BOATING LAKE

Queen Mary's Gardens

NASH TERRACES ★★

Holy Trinity

FITZROY

MARYLEBONE STATION

Rd

St. Marylebone

British Telecom Tower

Marylebone

MADAME TUSSAUD'S ★

ST. MARYLEBONE

St. Mary

All Souls Ch.

★★ **WALLACE COLLECTION**

Bryanston Sq.

Montagu Sq.

Wigmore

St.

Cavendish Sq.

George

★ **PORTMAN SQ.**

CITY OF WESTMINSTER

Selfridges

Seymour St.

Oxford

Oxford Circus

SO

Marble Arch

BOND

Bayswater

The Ring

Grosvenor Square

ST. ★

Pic Ci

MAYFAIR ★

Berkeley Square

MUSEUM OF MANKIND ★

HYDE **PARK** ★★

★ **BURLINGTON HOUSE**

★★ **BURLINGTON ARCADE**

★ J

Curzon St.

★ **ST. JAMES'S** ST.

★★ ST. J

★ **SHEPHERD MARKET**

PICCADILLY ★★

★★ ST. JA

♦ **QUEEN'S CHAPEL**

SERPENTINE

★★ **ST. JAMES'S PALACE**

★ **APSLEY HOUSE** (★ **WELLINGTON MUSEUM**)

Green Park

★ **LANCASTER HOUSE**

Carriage Road

Knightsbridge

Hyde Park Corner

Constitution Hill

ST. JA

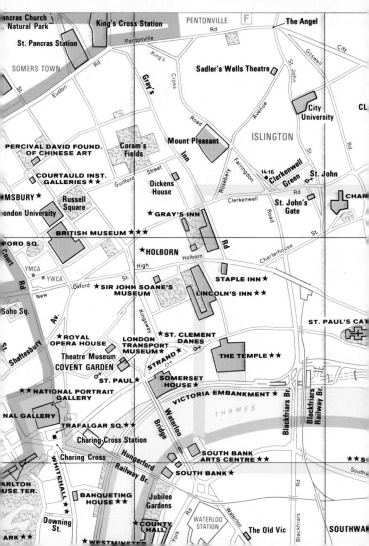

CENTRAL LONGON

CENTRAL LONDON

CENTRAL LONDON

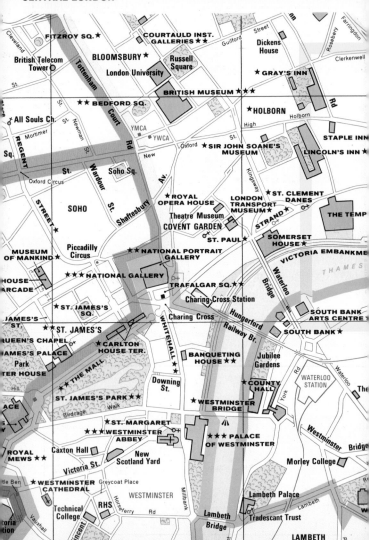

FITZROY SQ. ★

COURTAULD INST.
GALLERIES ★★

Cleveland

Farringdon

Street

Guilford

Roseberry

Dickens
House

Clerkenwell

British Telecom
Tower ○

BLOOMSBURY ★

Russell
Square

★ GRAY'S INN

London University

St.

Tottenham

★★ BEDFORD SQ. ★

BRITISH MUSEUM ★★★

Rd

★ HOLBORN

All Souls Ch. ★

Mortimer

Court

Newman

St.

St.

Holborn

STAPLE INN

REGENT

Wardour

YMCA

High

★ SIR JOHN SOANE'S
MUSEUM

LINCOLN'S INN

Sq.

St.

YWCA

Oxford

New

Oxford Circus

Soho Sq.

St.

Kingsway

★ ST. CLEMENT
DANES

SOHO

Shaftesbury

★ ROYAL
OPERA HOUSE

LONDON
TRANSPORT
MUSEUM

STREET ★

Theatre Museum

COVENT GARDEN

STRAND ★

THE TEMP

Piccadilly
Circus

★ ST. PAUL

SOMERSET
HOUSE ★

MUSEUM
OF MANKIND ★

★★ NATIONAL PORTRAIT
GALLERY

VICTORIA EMBANKME

HOUSE
ARCADE

★★★ NATIONAL GALLERY

THAMES

TRAFALGAR SQ. ★★

WHITEHALL

CHARING CROSS
Charing Cross Station

Waterloo

JAMES'S

★ ST. JAMES'S
SQ. ★

Charing Cross

Hungerford

Bridge

SOUTH BANK
ARTS CENTRE

ST.

★★ ST. JAMES'S

Railway Br.

SOUTH BANK

QUEEN'S CHAPEL

★ CARLTON
HOUSE TER.

★ BANQUETING
HOUSE ★★

Jubilee
Gardens

Rd

AMES'S PALACE

Waterloo

Park

★★ THE MALL

Downing
St.

★ COUNTY
HALL

WATERLOO
STATION

The

ER HOUSE

ST. JAMES'S PARK ★★

York

ACE

Hill

Birdcage

Walk

★ ST. MARGARET

★★★ WESTMINSTER
ABBEY

WESTMINSTER
BRIDGE

★★★ PALACE
OF WESTMINSTER

Westminster

Bridge

ROYAL
MEWS ★★

Caxton Hall

New
Scotland Yard

Morley College

tle Ben

★ WESTMINSTER
CATHEDRAL

Victoria St.

Greycoat Place

WESTMINSTER

Millbank

Rd

Technical
College

RHS

Horseferry

Rd

Lambeth Palace

oria
tion

Vincent

Vauxhall

Lambeth
Bridge

★ Tradescant Trust

Lambeth

LAMBETH

Rd

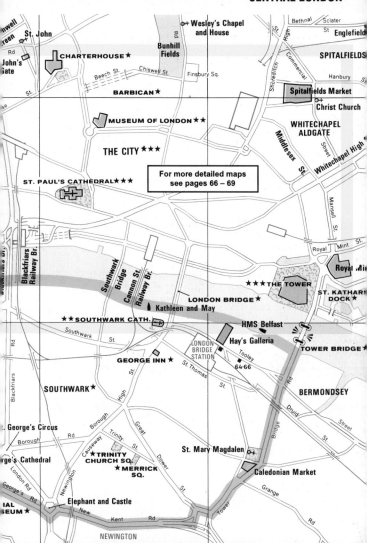

Wesley's Chapel and House

Bethnal · Sclater
St
Englefield

St. John

Bunhill Fields

SPITALFIELDS

John's Gate

CHARTERHOUSE ★

Beech St. Chiswell St. Finsbury Sq.

Hanbury

BARBICAN ★

Spitalfields Market

Christ Church

MUSEUM OF LONDON ★★

WHITECHAPEL ALDGATE

THE CITY ★★★

For more detailed maps see pages 66 – 69

ST. PAUL'S CATHEDRAL ★★★

Middlesex St.

Whitechapel High

Mansell St.

Royal Mint St.

Blackfriars Railway Br.

Royal Mi

★★★ THE TOWER

ST. KATHAR DOCK

Southwark Bridge

Cannon St. Railway Br.

LONDON BRIDGE ★

Kathleen and May

★★ SOUTHWARK CATH.

Southwark St.

HMS Belfast

Hay's Galleria

TOWER BRIDGE ★

Rd

LONDON BRIDGE STATION

Tooley

64-66

GEORGE INN ★

St. Thomas

St.

BERMONDSEY

SOUTHWARK ★

High

Druid

Blackfriars

Borough

Trinity

Great

Dover

. George's Circus

Borough Rd

St. Mary Magdalen

Bridge

Street

Causeway

★ TRINITY CHURCH SQ.

★ MERRICK SQ.

Caledonian Market

rge's Cathedral

London Rd

George's Rd

Newington

Elephant and Castle

Grange

IAL SEUM ★

New Kent Rd

Tower

Rd

NEWINGTON

PICCADILLY

● Start at **Piccadilly Circus** ☐ under the statue of **Eros** ☐ dedicated to the Earl of Shaftesbury for his charity work. Walk up **Piccadilly** ☐ which takes its name from *piccadil*, a collar fashionable in the seventeenth century. **St James's Church** ☐ on your left is next to the London Brass Rubbing Centre. ➡

Piccadilly Circus

Also on the left is Fortnum and Mason's famous provisions and general store founded in 1707. Every hour the founders emerge from the **Fortnum and Mason Clock** ☐ to see how trade is doing. Almost opposite is The Royal Academy of Arts in **Burlington House** ☐, and next to that **Burlington Arcade** ☐ with its exclusive shops patrolled by former 10th Hussars dressed as Regency beadles. Emma Hamilton gave birth to Lord Nelson's daughter at what is now **99 Piccadilly** ☐. ➡

Victoria Memorial

State Coach

The grand **Ritz** Hotel ☐, one of London's earliest steel-frame buildings, is next to **Green Park** ☐. Walk down through the park, as King Charles II was fond of doing. Soon you will see the **Victoria Memorial** ☐ in front of Her Majesty the Queen's London residence **Buckingham Palace** ☐. The Royal art collection can be seen in the **Queen's Gallery** ☐ and **state coaches** ☐ in the **Royal Mews** ☐. ➡

Buckingham Palace

Admiralty Arch

➡ Walk up **The Mall** ☐, with its distinctive red tarmac, leaving Buckingham Palace behind you. On the right is St James's Park (*see* page 25); on the left is Clarence House, home of the Queen Mother, and St James's Palace. Before you reach **Admiralty Arch** ☐, look out for the (Grand Old) **Duke of York's column** ☐ paid for by stopping a day's pay from every soldier in the British Army. Climb the steps into Carlton House Terrace to search out the former homes of **General de Gaulle** ☐ (while commanding the **Free French** ☐ during World War 2) and **Lord Kitchener** ☐ among others. ➡

The Athenaeum Club

Look for the **blue frieze** ☐ of the **Athenaeum Club** ☐ in Waterloo Place and the **Guards' Crimean Memorial** ☐ and **Florence Nightingale** ☐ across Pall Mall. The **guns** ☐ behind the memorial were captured from the Russians at Sebastopol; the figures were cast from melted-down Russian cannon. The tall modern building at the bottom of the Haymarket is **New Zealand House** ☐; this faces the **Theatre Royal** ☐ where *Tom Thumb* was first staged in 1730. ➡

Florence Nightingale and the Guards' Crimean Memorial

London Library

➡ Walking down **Pall Mall** ☐ away from **The Haymarket** ☐, you pass many of London's most famous clubs on your left. Next to the Athenaeum is the **Traveller's Club** ☐, and after that the **Reform** ☐. Opposite is a narrow street leading into **St James's Square** ☐. Look for the **London Library** ☐ in the far corner — it was founded by Thomas Carlyle in 1841. **No. 10** ☐ has been the home of three Prime Ministers and No. 4 has a plaque to **Nancy Astor** ☐ the first woman to become a Member of Parliament. Return to Pall Mall. There are more clubs on the far side as well as the former homes of the painter **Thomas Gainsborough** ☐ and **Nell Gwyn** ☐ (spelt Gwynne on the plaque), the seventeenth-century actress who became mistress to Charles II. ➡

At the bottom of St James's Street is the gateway to **St James's Palace** ☐. The poet Byron had lodgings in St James's Street which has many famous and long-established shops: **Berry Brothers and Rudd** ☐ (wine); **James Lock** ☐ (hats); and **Lobb** ☐ (boots). Regency dandies, including Beau Brummel, were among the regular customers. ➡

(Opposite) St James's Palace

➡ While in St James's, go into St James's Place. The nineteenth-century composer and pianist, Frédéric Chopin, left **No. 4** ☐ in 1848 to give his very last public performance. At the top of St James's, turn right into **Jermyn Street** ☐, which has a wonderful variety of traditional (and expensive) shops, many of them 'By Appointment' suppliers to the Queen and other members of the royal family. All of London's best shirtmakers are here, including **Turnbull & Asser** ☐. Your nose may lead you to **Floris** ☐ the perfumer, run by the same family since 1739. Equally delicious but rather different aromas come from the cheese shop **Paxton & Whitfield** ☐. ➡

Princes Arcade  will take you into Piccadilly. Cross over and go left, eventually turning up White Horse Street into **Shepherd Market** ☐. This delightful maze of alleys was designed by the builder Edward Shepherd in 1735; his home, **Crewe House** ☐, is a few paces north in Curzon Street. Here, in 1907, Sir Winston Churchill first met the woman who was to become his wife, his darling Clementine. Walk eastwards down **Curzon Street** ☐ looking for **Trumpers** ☐ where the aristocracy have been shaved and trimmed for generations. ➡

Princes Arcade (right)
Shepherd Market (below)

➡ From Curzon Street, go up Fitzmaurice Place into **Berkeley Square** ☐. You may not hear the nightingale of the song but there are many interesting houses. Clive of India died at **No. 45** ☐ in 1774 and Waldorf Astor and Gordon Selfridge both lived at **No. 54** ☐ — at different times. Go down Bruton Street. **No. 17** ☐ is now a bank but the house

Asprey

which stood on this site, and was destroyed by a bomb in 1940, was where the Queen was born on 21 April 1926. This leads into **Bond Street** ☐ where you will find many of London's most exclusive shops including **Asprey** ☐ the jewellers and **Sotheby's** ☐. ➡

Sotheby's

F D Roosevelt

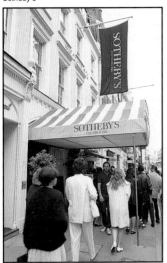

American Embassy (above)
Liberty (right)

From Bond Street you can walk down Brook Street past **Claridges Hotel** ☐ to Grosvenor Square to see the **American Embassy** ☐ and the statue of **F D Roosevelt** ☐ unveiled by his wife Eleanor in 1948. Return down Brook Street and pass **No. 25** ☐ where the composer Handel (1685-1759) wrote all his major works including the *Messiah*. Before reaching Regent Street, you will pass Hanover Square. The French statesman, Talleyrand-Périgord (1754-1838), known for his craftiness, lived at **No. 21** ☐. In Regent Street look for the world-famous shop **Liberty** ☐. ➡

➡ **Regent Street** ☐ was designed by John Nash (between 1813 and 1825) as part of the grand carriageway connecting the Prince Regent's residence, Carlton House, with Regent's Park. Look out for landmarks such as **Garrard** ☐, the Queen's jewellers, and the **Café Royal** ☐. ➡

The Palladium (above); Carnaby Street (above right); and the mural to Percy Bysshe Shelly, Poland Street (right)

From Liberty, go down Great Marlborough Street; the **Palladium** ☐ is off to the left and **Carnaby Street** ☐ to your right. Further on, at the corner of Noel Street and Poland Street, is the house where the poet, **Percy Bysshe Shelley** (1791-1822) ☐ lived. Another poet, **William Blake** (1757-1827) ☐, lived further down Poland Street and you will see his blue plaque on a modern building. Turn left at the bottom. At the end of Broadwick Street, you will see the (lunchtime) bustle of **Berwick Street Market** ☐ which sells some of the best fruit and vegetables in London, as well as cheese, shellfish and general merchandise. You are now in the heart of Soho. ➡

➡ **Soho** ☐ has some of the best restaurants and food shops in London. The unusual name of this area comes from a hunting call 'So-Ho!' rather like 'Tally-Ho!'. The shape of a fork with four prongs is a good way of picturing it as it is now: Wardour Street, Dean Street, Frith Street, and Greek Street, joined at the bottom by Old Compton Street. This probably makes **Soho Square** ☐ the green pea on the end of one prong! ➡

Soho Square

No. 163 Wardour Street ☐, itself the centre of the British Film Industry, was the home of Thomas Sheraton (1751-1806), the furniture maker. Dean Street is where **Karl Marx** ☐ began his writings on communism. ➡

Frith Street is famous for the world's first television demonstration by its inventor, the Scot, John Logie Baird (1888-1946), at **No. 22** ☐ in 1926, and also **Ronnie Scott's Jazz Club** ☐. Look for the well-known **Gay Hussar** ☐ Hungarian restaurant ☐ in Greek Street. ➡

Shaftesbury Avenue □, with its many theatres, runs parallel to Old Compton Street, and below that Gerrard Street the heart of London's **Chinatown** □. ■

The Palace Theatre (right); and Chinatown (below)

Trafalgar Square (above); dominated by Nelson's Column (below)

● **Trafalgar Square** ☐, named after Admiral Nelson's great naval victory over the Spanish and French fleets in 1805, is dominated by **Nelson's Column** ☐. The battle scenes at its base were cast from captured French cannon, **the Lions** ☐ from cannon of the *Royal George* which sank in 1782. ➡

The National Gallery

To the north of the Square is the **National Gallery** ☐ which houses one of the greatest collections of paintings in the world. Stand under its portico at the top of the steps. To your left is **St Martin-in-the-Fields** ☐ where King Charles II was baptized and his mistress, Nell Gwyn, buried. Straight ahead, across Trafalgar Square, you can see down Whitehall to the Houses of Parliament. Before that, on the south side of the Square, is the heart and official centre of London, **Charing Cross** ☐. Today, an equestrian statue of **Charles I** ☐ looks wistfully down Whitehall to where he was beheaded in 1660. Earlier, in 1291, Edward I had placed the last of thirteen crosses on the very same spot. The funeral procession for Eleanor of Castile had stretched from Nottinghamshire. This was the final memorial to his beloved Queen — his *chère Reine* cross. ➡

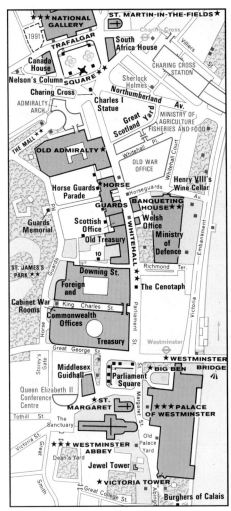

➡ **Whitehall** ☐ takes its name from Henry VIII's royal palace in which he married Anne Boleyn and where he died in 1547. Before walking down Whitehall from Trafalgar Square, you may want to see **Scotland Yard** ☐, the old headquarters of the Metropolitan Police, and close by **The Sherlock Holmes pub** ☐. In Whitehall, before you reach the Banqueting House, you will see the huge buildings of the **War Office** ☐, now part of the Ministry of Defence. Opposite is **Horse Guards** ☐ with its clock tower and guard mounted by the Household Cavalry. If possible, walk through here to **Horse Guards Parade** ☐ where the trooping of the colour takes place. ➡

Horse Guards

Nearby are the **Cabinet War Rooms** ☐ and, beyond, **St James's Park** ☐, the most beautiful in London. Alongside is **Birdcage Walk** ☐ named after Charles II's aviary. Back in Whitehall, take time to look at the **Banqueting House** ☐, a masterpiece by the English architect, Inigo Jones (1573-1652), with a ceiling painted by the Flemish painter Rubens (1577-1640). The bust of Charles I marks the position of the window the King stepped through on to the scaffold in 1649; Charles I 'who never said a foolish thing, nor ever did a wise one'. On the other side of Whitehall is **Downing Street** ☐ and, in the centre, the **Cenotaph** ☐ commemorating those servicemen and women who have died in war. ➡

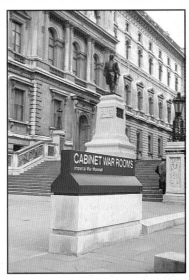

St James's Park

➡ Before entering **Parliament Square** ☐, walk out on to **Westminster Bridge** ☐ for one of the best views of the **Houses of Parliament** ☐. The proper title 'Palace of Westminster' comes from the fact that this was the site of the sovereign's main London residence from Saxon times until 1529 when Henry VIII took Whitehall from Cardinal Wolsey. The present building was opened by Queen Victoria in 1852. The **Victoria Tower** ☐ is the tallest stone square tower in the world at over 102 metres (336 ft), although the Clock Tower is more famous. **Big Ben** ☐, as the Clock Tower is often known, is really the 13½-ton bell cast at Whitechapel (*see* page 78). It is Big Ben's voice which marks the passing of the hours in London. ➡

Boudicca (above); Houses of Parliament (opposite); and Sir Winston Churchill (right)

Returning to Parliament Square you will pass the statue of **Boudicca** □ (Boadicea) driving her own answer to London's traffic. **Sir Winston Churchill** (1874-1965) □ dominates the green much as he did the Commons in his lifetime but there are many other interesting statues. On the far side is **Middlesex Guildhall** □, to the left **St Margaret's Church** □. ➡

➡ No building has more to tell of English history than **Westminster Abbey** ☐. It has seen the coronation of every monarch since William the Conqueror and contains memorials to many of the nation's great men and women. The first recorded church on the site was built before AD 750 but the present structure is medieval. The **nave** ☐ was built in the late fourteenth century by the mysterious architect Henry Yevele. The most important addition since then was **Henry VII's Chapel** ☐. Of all the Abbey's numerous memorials, the most moving is the grave of the **Unknown Warrior** ☐. Truly unknown, he was buried with the highest honours in 1921 and lies in soil brought from the battlefield: an anonymous representative of more than a million men who gave their lives in World War 1. ➡

The nave (above left); and Henry VII's Chapel (left), Westminster Abbey

Outside again, look for the dome of **Methodist Central Hall** ☐ and seek out the peace of **Dean's Yard** ☐ and the **Abbey Garden** ☐. Return to **Palace Yard** ☐ where **Oliver Cromwell** ☐ presides over the Parliament he gave life to. On the same spot Guy Fawkes and other Gunpowder Plot conspirators had their lives taken away. **Victoria Tower Gardens** ☐ are interesting. There is a statue of **Emmeline Pankhurst** ☐, who fought for women's rights, and a statue by Rodin of the heroic **Burghers of Calais** ☐. ➡

➡ From Parliament Square a long walk or a short bus ride down Victoria Street will bring you to **Westminster Cathedral** ☐, England's principal Roman Catholic church, consecrated in 1910. From the bell tower (campanile) there are wonderful views of London. On a clear day it is possible to see the North Downs and Crystal Palace to the south and Harrow and Hampstead to the north. The campanile is 83 metres (273 ft) high, but there is a lift! The cross on top of Westminster Cathedral contains a relic of the True Cross. ➡

The Tate Gallery (above) Westminster Cathedral (opposite)

A different route, walking along the river from Parliament Square, will take you down Millbank, passing **Lambeth Bridge** ☐ and the headquarters of **ICI** ☐. Next is **Millbank Tower** ☐ built for Vickers in 1963, and the **Tate Gallery** ☐. Built originally through the generosity of the sugar magnate, Sir Henry Tate, the gallery houses a magnificent collection of modern painting and sculpture. Look for Rodin's *The Kiss* ☐. ■

● Starting at Victoria **Station** ☐, you can go either down to the Embankment and the river or head across to Belgravia and Knightsbridge. For Belgravia, find Eccleston Street. You may be interested to cross the bridge to find Eccleston Square where the **Churchills** ☐ lived after their marriage; otherwise, cross Buckingham

Victoria main line Station

Palace Road and go up Eccleston Street. Ebury Street is full of interest. At the age of 8, the Austrian composer, Wolfgang Amadeus Mozart (1756-91) completed his first symphony at **No. 180** ☐. At **No. 111** ☐ the mother of a different prodigy, Noel Coward, took in lodgers. In Chester Square, Mary Shelley, author of *Frankenstein*, died at **No. 24** ☐. At Eaton Square you can turn left down to Sloane Square, the **Royal Court Theatre** ☐, and on to **King's Road** ☐ and Chelsea. ➡

Or you can carry on to Belgrave Square to find the signature of George Basevi on **No. 37** ☐. He was the architect employed by Thomas Cubitt to design most of the fine squares in this most fashionable area of London. From Belgrave Square go down Chesham Place, crossing Sloane Street with its smart shops, into Pont Street and Beauchamp Place (pronounced 'Beecham'). From here you can go up to Knightsbridge and **Harrods** ☐ or left down Walton Street (P G Wodehouse lived at **No. 16** ☐) to the art deco **Michelin House** ☐ in Fulham Road. ■

Michelin House

33

Between Teddington Lock and the Tower of London, there are no less than twenty-eight road, railway, and foot bridges across the River Thames. **Richmond Bridge** ☐ is the oldest and was built in 1774. It is a classical stone bridge on which a toll was charged until the middle of the nineteenth century. Then, going down river, come **Richmond Railway Bridge** ☐, **Twickenham Bridge** ☐, and **Richmond Footbridge** ☐. **Kew Bridge** ☐ is another attractive stone bridge built in 1903 to replace an earlier structure. Next is **Kew Railway Bridge** ☐ followed by **Chiswick Bridge** ☐ and **Barnes Railway Bridge** ☐ — this is an iron bridge with a unique humpback outline. **Hammersmith Bridge** ☐ is a suspension bridge completed in 1887 while **Putney Bridge** ☐, built of Cornish granite, is the starting point for the annual Oxford and Cambridge boat race. Next come **Fulham Railway Bridge** ☐,

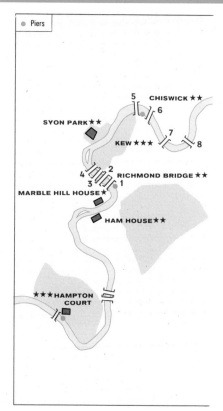

● Piers

CHISWICK ★★
SYON PARK ★★
KEW ★★★
RICHMOND BRIDGE ★★
MARBLE HILL HOUSE ★
HAM HOUSE ★★
★★★ HAMPTON COURT

Wandsworth Bridge ☐, and **Battersea Railway Bridge** ☐, which is the only bridge to carry a railway line directly connecting southern and northern England. The decoratively painted **Battersea Bridge** ☐ is next followed by the suspension cantilever **Albert Bridge** ☐, which is lit up at night. Further down the river are **Chelsea Bridge** ☐, **Victoria Railway Bridge** ☐, **Vauxhall Bridge** ☐, and **Lambeth Bridge** ☐ with its red and black parapet. **Westminster Bridge** ☐ is a seven-arched stone-built bridge completed in 1862 and is where William Wordsworth wrote his famous sonnet. **Hungerford Bridge** ☐, more properly known as Charing Cross Railway Bridge with its parallel

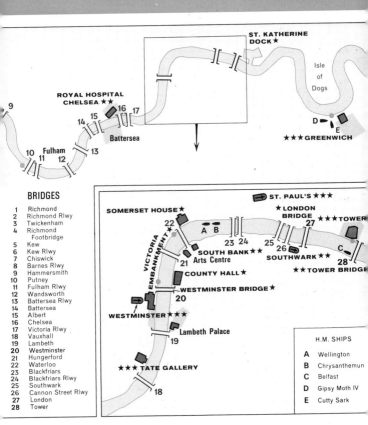

ST. KATHERINE DOCK ★

Isle of Dogs

ROYAL HOSPITAL
CHELSEA ★★

Battersea

D
★★★ GREENWICH
E

9

14 15 16 17

10 Fulham 13

11 12

BRIDGES

1	Richmond
2	Richmond Rlwy
3	Twickenham
4	Richmond Footbridge
5	Kew
6	Kew Rlwy
7	Chiswick
8	Barnes Rlwy
9	Hammersmith
10	Putney
11	Fulham Rlwy
12	Wandsworth
13	Battersea Rlwy
14	Battersea
15	Albert
16	Chelsea
17	Victoria Rlwy
18	Vauxhall
19	Lambeth
20	**Westminster**
21	Hungerford
22	Waterloo
23	Blackfriars
24	Blackfriars Rlwy
25	Southwark
26	Cannon Street Rlwy
27	London
28	Tower

ST. PAUL'S ★★★

SOMERSET HOUSE ★
22
★ LONDON BRIDGE ★★★ TOWER
27
A B
23 24 25 26
SOUTH BANK ★★ C
Arts Centre SOUTHWARK ★★ 28
21
VICTORIA EMBANKMENT
★★ TOWER BRIDGE
COUNTY HALL ★

WESTMINSTER BRIDGE ★
20

WESTMINSTER ★★★

Lambeth Palace
19

★★★ TATE GALLERY

18

H.M. SHIPS	
A	Wellington
B	Chrysanthemun
C	Belfast
D	Gipsy Moth IV
E	Cutty Sark

footbridge, is next, and then there are **Waterloo Bridge** ☐, **Blackfriars Bridge** ☐, and **Blackfriars Railway Bridge** ☐. **Southwark Bridge** ☐ is called the 'Cast Iron Bridge' in Charles Dickens's *Little Dorrit*. Then comes the vast **Cannon Street Railway Bridge** ☐. Today's **London Bridge** ☐ is a concrete construction, built in 1973 to replace the old London Bridge which was dismantled and shipped to the United States. Last, but by no means least, is the famous **Tower Bridge** ☐, built in 1894 and having an iron drawbridge which can be raised by power mechanisms contained within the towers. A new bridge is under construction at Dartford.

Chelsea Bridge (above); Battersea Power Staion (below)

● From Victoria Station, turn left down Buckingham Palace Road to **Chelsea Bridge** ☐. Across the Thames is the redundant **Battersea Power Station** ☐ (the 'inverted grand piano') and above you to the left the **shot tower** ☐ where lead shot was made by pouring the molten metal through a seive and then allowing it fall into a tank of cold water so that it forms spheres. From Chelsea Bridge, go up Chelsea Bridge Road and turn left into Royal Hospital Road. To your left are the grounds of the Royal Hospital where the Chelsea Flower Show is held each year. Sir Christopher Wren (1632-1723) was the architect of the Royal (or Chelsea) Hospital which was founded by Charles II in 1682 for veteran and invalid soldiers. If you turn right into Franklin's Row and left into St Leonard's Terrace for the view through the fine wrought iron gates of what was once the main entrance to the **Royal Hospital** ☐, you may spot the former residence of **Bram Stoker** ☐, author of *Dracula* ➡

Bram Stoker's house (far left); the Royal Hospital (below)

The Shot Tower

Further on, look out for the **Victorian pillar box** ☐ with its pagoda-like top.
Returning to the main road, you will come to the **National Army Museum** ☐.
Turn left into Tite Street a little further on and you can find the house where
Oscar Wilde ☐ lived. Continue past the house and turn right into Dilke
Street; walk along to **Swan Walk** ☐ and the **Chelsea Physic Garden** ☐. This
ancient apothecaries' garden is sometimes open to the public. Even if it is
not, peer through the gates and reflect that the very first cotton seeds were
taken from this little garden to America in 1732. ➡

➡ **Cheyne Walk** ☐ (pronounced 'chainy') has some of the most attractive Georgian houses in London. Many notable people have lived in this exclusive row, including the novelist **George Eliot** ☐ at No. 4, the statesman David Lloyd-George (1863-1945) at **No. 10** ☐, and the painter Dante Gabriel Rossetti ((1828-82) at **No. 16** ☐ with a menagerie in the garden. Further along, **Albert Bridge** ☐ is particularly fine. Look out for the statue of the Victorian author, **Thomas Carlyle** ☐, and turn up Cheyne Row to find his **house** ☐. ➡

You can then turn into Lawrence Street to look for the plaque which marks the site of the **Chelsea Pottery** ☐ where the novelist, Tobias Smollett also lived. Back on the riverside there is an interesting monument to **Sir Joseph William Bazalgette** ☐, the engineer of the Chelsea Embankment who also constructed the main sewage system of London. Nearby, and close to the site of his former house, is a statue of **Sir Thomas More** ☐ who was martyred by Henry VIII. Look out for **house boats** ☐ moored along the Embankment. Towards the end of Cheyne Walk is **No. 119** ☐, where the artist, Joseph Turner died in 1851. He was perhaps the greatest painter of light there has ever been; curiously, although it was a foggy December morning, it is recorded that a shaft of sunlight flooded his little attic room at the moment of his death. ■

● **Hyde Park Corner** ☐ is the busiest junction in London so use the pedestrian subways. You can almost imagine that the roar of the cars is the sound of battle, because this is a very military place. There are memorials to the **Royal Artillery** ☐ and to the **Machine Gun Corps** ☐, but the dominating presence is of the 'Iron Duke' of Wellington. The **Wellington Arch** ☐ at the centre was erected in 1828, and there is a statue of the Duke mounted on his war horse **Copenhagen** ☐ in front of **Apsley House** ☐ (always known as No. 1 London) which was his London home for many years. ➡

*Achilles (above); and Jacob
Epstein's Devil (right)*

Behind that, and close to the entrance to **Hyde Park** ☐, looms the gigantic
figure of one of the legendary Greek heroes from Homer's *Iliad*, **Achilles** ☐,
made from melted-down French cannon and dedicated by 'their
countrywomen' to Wellington and his soldiers. Three paths lead into Hyde
Park (from right to left) **Serpentine Road** ☐, sandy **Rotten Row** ☐ (so called
from the French *Route du Roi* — 'King's Way') for riders, and the **Carriage-
way** ☐ which can be joined from Knightsbridge where you might see Jacob
Epstein's **Devil** ☐ pursuing others into the park. From Apsley House, take the
Serpentine Road (once called Ladies' Mile) past the Dell and alongside the
Serpentine ☐. To your right was the site of the Great Exhibition of 1851.
Follow the paths, or make your own way round to Marble Arch at the top of
Park Lane. ➡

➡ **Marble Arch** ☐ (use the pedestrian subway) was originally intended to be the main gate to Buckingham Palace but, because it proved to be too narrow for the King's Coach, it was moved. Its present site has a ghastly history. This was Tyburn, for 600 years London's public execution place. The position of the permanent gallows, '**Tyburn Tree**' ☐, is marked by a stone on the island opposite Edgware Road. Countless men and women — highwaymen and priests, the good and the bad — were hanged and mutilated here. ➡

Marble Arch (above); Speakers' Corner (left); and paintings in Bayswater Road (bottom)

After the Restoration of the monarchy in 1660, Oliver Cromwell was exhumed from Westminster Abbey, displayed on a gibbet, beheaded, and finally buried at the foot of the gallows. Despite these indignities, the Lord Protector would have been pleased to see the democratic freedom exercised at **Speakers' Corner** ☐ just inside Hyde Park. Generally less grisly, too, are the **paintings displayed on the railings** ☐ a little way down the Bayswater Road. ➡

North Ride (above); The Dorchester hotel (right); and the London Hilton (below)

Unless you want to see **North Ride** ☐, in the part of the park famous for duels in the eighteenth century, walk down **Park Lane** ☐. Most of the great mansions are now gone or have been replaced by grand hotels. Lord Louis Mountbatten once lived at **No. 36** ☐ and Benjamin Disraeli at **No. 93** ☐. Also look for **The Dorchester** ☐ and the **London Hilton** ☐ before returning to Hyde Park Corner. ■

● Although several of London's Museums are close together, it is a mistake to try to see too much at once. It is an interesting part of town so you can add variety to each visit. Start from **South Kensington Underground** ☐ and walk northwards. At the **Ismaili Centre** ☐, built by the Aga Khan Foundation, turn right into Cromwell Road to see **Brompton Oratory** ☐, a famous Roman Catholic church. Look for the statue of **Cardinal Newman** ☐. Returning along Cromwell Road, you will see in the middle of the road one of the interesting **cab shelters** ☐ used by London's cab drivers for many years and now preserved. By now you will be standing by the entrance to the **Victoria and Albert Museum** ☐ which houses an incomparable collection of art and decoration from all countries and periods. Cross **Exhibition Road** ☐ and you will come to the **Natural History Museum** ☐ with its unrivalled archive of specimens and, of course, its dinosaurs. ➡

Brompton Oratory (opposite top); a cab shelter (opposite bottom); the Victoria and Albert Museum (above left); the Royal Academy of Music (above right); and the Natural History Museum (right)

Before going up Exhibition Road, you may like to see the **headquarters of the Scout Association** ☐ and memorial to **Lord Baden-Powell** ☐ further on. On the south side is the **French Lycée** ☐. In Exhibition Road you will find the **Geological Museum** ☐ and the **Science Museum** ☐. Further up, look out for the **Royal College of Music** ☐ to the left in Prince Consort Road. ➡

The Royal Geographical Society

➡ At the top of Exhibition Road, you may find the British Antarctic explorer, **Sir Ernest Shackleton** (1874-1922) ☐, sheltering in an alcove in the wall of the **Royal Geographical Society** ☐, with **David Livingstone** (1813-73) ☐ for company nearby. Look out here, too, for an interesting cast metal **mile post** ☐.Turning left into **Kensington Gore** ☐, you will see the **Royal Albert Hall** ☐. This is where the famous Promenade Concerts ('the Proms') begun by Sir Henry Wood (1869-1944) are held each year. ➡

The Royal Albert Hall

Kensington Gardens (above); and Peter Pan (right)

Opposite, in **Kensington Gardens** ☐, is the **Albert Memorial** ☐: the controversial monument Queen Victoria had built after the death of her beloved consort Prince Albert. If you look closely, you will see that the Prince is holding the catalogue of the Great Exhibition of 1851. Kensington Gardens is quite different in mood from Hyde Park. This is the magical world of **Peter Pan** ☐ and you will find the statue of J M Barrie's character, the boy who remains eternally young, by the **Long Water** ☐. Make your way to the edge of the Gardens where you can glimpse Wren's **Kensington Palace** ☐ and the **Orangery** ☐. Queen Victoria was born in Kensington Palace in 1819 and lived there until she ascended the throne in 1827. The State Apartments and magnificent Court Dress Collection are well worth seeing before leaving the Gardens. ■

The Orangery

Broadcasting House (above); Telecom Tower (left)

● From Oxford Circus Underground ☐, walk northwards up Regent Street. Where the road curves at Langham Place, you will see the circular front of **All Souls Church** ☐ built by John Nash and, behind it, **Broadcasting House** ☐. Over the main door, look for **the frieze** ☐ by the controversial sculptor Eric Gill (1882-1940). Go up Riding House Street in front of All Souls and walk up to Cleveland Street, looking out for the **Telecom Tower** [177 metres (580 ft)] ☐. You are now in the heart of Fitzrovia which is full of interest, both for the people who have lived there and for the story its street names tell. The Duchess of Cleveland (born Barbara Villiers 1641-1709) had several children by Charles II: all these were called 'Fitzroy', One son, Henry, was made Earl of Euston and then Duke of Grafton. He acquired by marriage a huge estate in the area around Tottenham Court Road which was developed much as you see it today. Charles Dickens (1812-70) lived at **No. 22 Cleveland Street** ☐

in 1830, and the painters Rossetti, Holman Hunt, and Millais founded the Pre-Raphaelite Brotherhood at **No. 7** ☐ in 1848. At the bottom end of Cleveland Street, cross into Charlotte Street, now famous for its restaurants and once the home of the painter John Constable (1776-1837) at **No. 95** ☐. A short detour into parallel Whitfield Street to see **Pollock's Toy Museum** ☐ is worthwhile. ➡

Robert Stephenson (above); King's Cross station (right).

Walk northwards in Charlotte Street until you come to Fitzroy Square. George Bernard Shaw (1856-1950) lived here with his mother (at **No. 29** ☐); the novelist, Virginia Woolf (1882-1941), with her brother in the same house later. From Fitzroy Square, go north into Euston Road and turn right to see three of London's great stations. You will see **Euston** ☐ first. Look for the statue of the railway engineer **Robert Stephenson** ☐ in the forecourt, and **Friends House** ☐, the headquarters of the Quakers, in Euston Square. Continue east along Euston Road until you see **St Pancras** ☐, romantic and extravagant compared with the functional **King's Cross** ☐ next door but both wonderful examples of Victorian architecture. The **King's Cross Clock** ☐ was taken from the original Crystal Palace of the Great Exhibition of 1851. From King's Cross you can use the underground to return to Oxford Circus. ■

St Pancras station

PORTLAND PLACE/HARLEY STREET

● From Oxford Circus, walk northwards up Regent Street, past the BBC into Portland Place. The novelist and crime writer, Edgar Wallace (1875-1932) lived at **No. 31** ☐. Look for the statue of the famous surgeon, **Lord Lister** (1827-1912) ☐, and his home at **No. 12 Park Crescent** ☐ — Lister was the first person to use antiseptics in surgery. On the corner of Park Crescent is a bust of **John F Kennedy** ☐. Turn left into Marylebone Road. Almost immediately on your left you will see **Harley Street** ☐ where many of Britain's finest doctors have consulting rooms. If you feel like a detour, the British statesman Gladstone (1809-98) lived at **No. 73** ☐; the painter Turner lived at **No. 45** ☐ at the height of his popularity; the playwright, Sir Arthur Wing Pinero (1855-1934), at No. **15A** ☐, and, from **No. 11** ☐, plain Sir Arthur Wellesley (later Duke of Wellington) left to find fame and fortune in the Peninsular War (1808-14). Back in Marylebone Road, you will soon come to **Madame Tussaud's waxworks exhibition** ☐, and the **London Planetarium** ☐. ➡

A trip by llama carriage, London Zoo (above); and a bandstand in Regent's Park (right)

Just before that is York Gate, the way into **Regent's Park** ☐. You must decide how to explore the Park and in what order. Going left round the Outer Circle will take you past Hanover Terrace where Dickens wrote *Great Expectations* at **No. 3** ☐, and where the English novelist, H G Wells (1866-1946), lived (**No. 13** ☐), on to the **London Central Mosque** ☐, and finally to the **London Zoo** ☐. After that the Outer Circle returns past Nash's superb **Cumberland Terrace** ☐ to the top of Great Portland Street and to where you began at Oxford Circus. But, if you go straight on from York Gate, you will come to the Inner Circle with **Queen Mary's Gardens** ☐ and the **Open Air Theatre** ☐. You can also take a pleasure boat on the Regent's Canal to Little Venice and Paddington (*see* page 52). ∎

Madame Tussaud's and the London Planetarium (opposite); Cumberland Terrace (right)

● Start at **Paddington Station** ☐ or **Little Venice** ☐ if you have come by boat on **Regent's Canal** ☐ from Regent's Park, making your way by under-ground to the station which is the terminus of Brunel's Great Western Railway. In Praed Street, you may like to see **St Mary's Hospital** ☐ where **Sir Alexander Fleming** (1881-1955) ☐ discovered penicillin. This was where the sons of the present Prince and Princess of Wales were born. Take the underground to **Edgware Road** ☐ which was the Roman Watling Street and walk (or bus) down to the end of Seymour Street just before Marble Arch. ➡

Little Venice (above); the crest above Paddington station (below)

Edward Lear (1812-88), inventor of the nonsense limerick, lived at **No. 30 Seymour Street** . To the north, and parallel, is George Street where — at **No. 5 Bryanston Court** □ — Edward VIII and Mrs Simpson used to meet. Keep walking eastwards until you come to Baker Street. There is no '221B' but the house Sir Arthur Conan Doyle (1859-1930) chose for Sherlock Holmes was **No. 21**. Go down Baker Street into Oxford Street to find **Selfridges** □, and then up Duke Street to Manchester Square for the **Wallace Collection** □, perhaps the finest art collection ever donated by a private individual. Leave Manchester Square the way you entered and turn left along Wigmore Street past **Wigmore Hall** □. ➡

THE WALLACE COLLECTION
OPEN: MONDAY TO SATURDAY 10-5 SUNDAY 2-5
CLOSED: NEW YEAR'S DAY, GOOD FRIDAY, MAY DAY BANK HOLIDAY, CHRISTMAS EVE, CHRISTMAS DAY AND BOXING DAY   ADMISSION FREE

On your way to Regent Street and Oxford Circus, take time to walk up **Wimpole Street** □. At No. 50 (now rebuilt) lived the Barretts. Of the poet Robert Browning, whom she married, the daughter of the house, Elizabeth, whose room was on the third floor, was later to write 'How do I love thee? Let me count the ways...'. They eloped on 20 September 1846. ■

WIMPOLE
STREET W1
CITY OF WESTMINSTER

● Start at Tottenham Court Road Underground. Go down **Charing Cross Road** ☐, famous for its bookshops, and look for Flitcroft Street on the left by the **Phoenix Theatre** ☐. Follow the narrow alley to **St Giles-in-the-Fields** ☐, once on the route to Tyburn and built by Henry Flitcroft. From here walk up St Giles High Street and turn right into New Oxford Street. Carry on past **James Smith & Sons** ☐, the stick and umbrella shop, and into Bloomsbury Way. You will see Museum Street on the left. At the top is the **British Museum** ☐, the most comprehensive and richest collection of its kind in the world. Coming from the front entrance of the British Museum turn right, then right again into **Bloomsbury** ☐. This leads to **Bedford Square** ☐ once famous for its publishers. Turn right along Montague Place to Russell Square. The Pankhursts, who fought for women's rights, lived at **No. 8** ☐. ➡

The British Museum

The famous Lamb pub

Look at the wonderful **Russell Hotel** ☐, then go along Guildford Street. On the left you will soon see **Coram's Fields** ☐ where Thomas Coram, with help from the composer Handel and Hogarth the painter, founded his hospital (now moved) to care for children. Down Lamb's Conduit Street, past the famous **Lamb** ☐ pub is **Great Ormonde Street** ☐ where they still care for children. Doughty Street crosses Guildford Street further along; here, at No. 48, is **The Dickens House** ☐. Close by is the Gray's Inn Road. Turn right and go past **Gray's Inn** ☐ itself until you come to Holborn. Go left here and explore **Leather Lane Market** ☐, and **Hatton Garden** ☐ which is the next turning on the left. This is the centre of the diamond business. Look for **Ye Olde Mitre** ☐ public house, first established in 1546. Back down Holborn the opposite way, just past Chancery Lane on the left is **Lincoln's Inn** ☐, one of London's four Inns of Court. Every barrister in England and Wales must belong to Inner or Middle Temple, Gray's or Lincoln's Inn, to be able to practise law. ■

Leather Lane Market (above); Lincoln's Inn (below)

Bush House (top); the Law Courts (above); St Clement Danes church (above right); and The Wig & Pen Club (below)

● Start at Holborn Underground and visit the fascinating **Sir John Soane's Museum** ☐ at Lincoln's Inn before walking down Kingsway to the crescent of the **Aldwych** ☐. Here you will see **India House** ☐, **Bush House** ☐, which is the headquarters of the BBC World Service, and **Australia House** ☐. Going east, you will see in the middle of the road **St Clement Danes** ☐, the church of the Royal Air Force with the famous peal 'Oranges and Lemons say the Bells of St Clement's!' Beyond and on the left are the **Law Courts** ☐. Look for **Twining's** ☐ the tea merchants on the opposite side, and **The Wig & Pen Club** ☐, the only Strand building to escape the Great Fire of 1666. A few paces more bring you to **Temple Bar** ☐ which is the beginning of the City. Even now, on State occasions, the Queen asks formal permission to enter the City just as Elizabeth I did. In the Middle Ages, the heads of traitors on spikes marked the spot; today there is only the **griffin** ☐. ➡

No. 1 Fleet Street is **Child's Bank** ☐, the oldest in London: Charles II, Nell Gwyn, and Samuel Pepys were all customers. On the other side of Fleet Street beyond Fetter Lane is a series of historic 'courts' which it is fun to explore: **Crane Court** ☐ where the magazine *Punch* was first published; **Red Lion Court** ☐; **Johnson's Court** ☐ where you can see **Dr Johnson's House** ☐ (Dr Johnson — 1709-84 — was compiler of the first English dictionary); **St Dunstan's Court** ☐; **Bolt Court** ☐; **Hind Court** ☐; and **Wine Office Court** ☐ where you will find the **Old Cheshire Cheese** ☐ pub. At the end of Fleet Street, turn right into New Bridge Street. Just before the bridge, on the other side, you will see the **Black Friar** ☐ pub which is full of fascinating decoration. Recross New Bridge Street and walk down the Embankment, taking the third turning on the right. You can now explore the tranquillity of the **Temple** ☐ and find the round **Temple Church** ☐ built by the mysterious Knights Templar in 1185. One of those suspected of being Jack the Ripper lived in **King's Bench Walk** ☐, so just have a quick look before making your way up Middle Temple Lane and back into Fleet Street! ■

The Black Friar pub (above); and Dr Johnson's House (right)

London does not have a 'theatreland' in quite the same way as some cities. As you will see from the map, there are theatres all over the West End and beyond. Londoners are very fortunate to have such a wealth of live entertainment and so many theatres and concert halls to choose from. How many have you visited?

1	Adelphi	☐	22	Her Majesty's	☐
2	Albery	☐	23	Lyric	☐
3	Aldwych	☐	24	Lyric Hammersmith	☐
4	Ambassadors	☐	25	Mayfair	☐
5	Apollo	☐	26	Mermaid	☐
6	Apollo Victoria	☐	27	National Film Theatre	☐
7	Arts Theatre	☐	28	National Theatre	☐
8	Barbican Centre	☐	29	New London	☐
9	Cambridge	☐	30	Old Vic	☐
10	Cochrane	☐	31	Palace	☐
11	Coliseum	☐	32	Palladium	☐
12	Comedy	☐	33	Phoenix	☐
13	Covent Garden	☐	34	Piccadilly	☐
14	Criterion	☐	35	Players	☐
15	Drury Lane	☐	36	Playhouse	☐
16	Duchess	☐	37	Prince Edward	☐
17	Duke of York's	☐	38	Prince of Wales	☐
18	Fortune	☐	39	Purcell Room	☐
19	Garrick	☐	39	Queen Elizabeth Hall	☐
20	Globe	☐	40	Queen's	☐
21	Haymarket	☐	41	Round House	☐

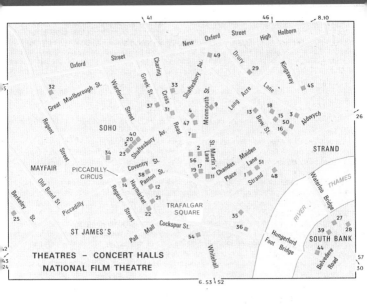

The National Theatre (opposite); and the Cambridge Theatre (right)

The offices of The Lady *(above); and Rules restaurant (below)*

● Start at Leicester Square Underground. Walk eastwards, crossing St Martin's Lane. A pleasant detour is to go down St Martin's Lane a little way to browse in the Aladdin's cave of **Cecil Court** ☐. Otherwise go down Garrick Street; on the right is the **Garrick Club** ☐ which has many actors and writers as members. Walk down Bedford Street, past the offices of *The Lady* ☐ magazine and turn into **Maiden Lane** ☐. This is not so ladylike — in the 1630s, it was called Midden Lane, meaning dungheap! However, at **No. 9** ☐, the French historian and essayist, François Voltaire ((1694-1788) once lived in exile and J M W Turner, perhaps the greatest painter England ever produced, was born and raised over his father's hairdresser's shop at **No. 26** ☐ — the old building has now gone. Look out for **Rules** ☐, one of the oldest restaurants in London. ➡

Turn left at Southampton Street into **Covent Garden** ☐. This was the city's fruit and vegetable market for 300 years but is now full of shops, stalls, and **street entertainers** ☐. To the west of the market square is the 'actors church' **St Paul's** ☐. Under its portico, George Bernard Shaw's Eliza Doolittle was selling flowers when she was first spotted by 'Enry 'Iggins. See if you can find the memorial to the English composer, **Thomas Arne** ☐, who died in 1798 — he wrote *Rule Britannia*. On the south side of the square is the **London Transport Museum** ☐ full of wonderful things to see and operate. ➡

Inside Covent Garden (above right); and the London Transport Museum (right)

BOW STREET/ROYAL OPERA HOUSE/DRURY LANE

➡ In Covent Garden, leave the market square and turn left up **Bow Street** ☐. At the top is the **Royal Opera House** ☐. The list of great singers and dancers who have performed here would fill a book. You may be lucky enough to hear the singers rehearsing from the little alley which runs up the side of the Opera House. Nearly opposite is

Bow Street Magistrate's Court ☐. The first magistrate to preside here, in 1748, was Henry Fielding who wrote *Tom Jones*. Walk up Broad Court, where there is a figure of a **dancer** ☐, into Great Queen Street where you cannot miss **Freemason's Hall** ☐ with its 60-metre (200-ft) tower. Retrace your steps and go down **Drury Lane** ☐ to see the **Theatre Royal** ☐ — the largest in London and the fourth to be built on the same site. Turn up Russell Street to look into the charming **Fortune Theatre** ☐. ➡

The Royal Opera House

Turn left into Wellington Street opposite the entrance to Covent Garden Market, to reach Aldwych and the Strand, perhaps pausing in Tavistock Street to see where **Thomas de Quincy** ☐ wrote the classic *Confessions of an Opium Eater.* ■

Theatre Royal (above); and the Fortune Theatre (below)

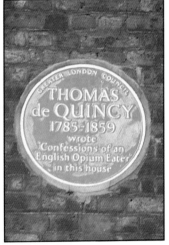

STRAND

● Start at Embankment Underground, and walk northwards away from the river into **Villiers Street** ☐. Before the railway was built in 1864, the area to the left was Hungerford Market, the site of the terrible blacking factory where Charles Dickens worked as a boy. The nearby footbridge across the Thames is still called **Hungerford Bridge** ☐. Further up Villiers Street on the right is **Gordon's Wine Bar** ☐, one of the oldest in London. Climb the stairs to the Strand. To the left, in front of Charing Cross Station, is a Victorian reconstruction of how the original **Charing Cross** ☐ may have looked. Turn right down the Strand ('strand' means 'riverbank' and, in the Middle Ages, there was nothing between this road and the Thames). On your right you will pass the interesting **Coal Hole** ☐ pub, a favourite of the Welsh poet Dylan Thomas (1914-53). Next, on the same side, is the entrance to the grand **Savoy Hotel** ☐, and the **Savoy Theatre** ☐. ➡

A reconstruction of the original Charing Cross (above)

CLEOPATRA'S NEEDLE

Further on is **Simpsons Restaurant** ☐, famous for its traditional English food. Across the approach to Waterloo Bridge is **Somerset House** ☐ which now houses the Courtauld Collection of art. Return from this point by descending the steps by the side of Waterloo Bridge and walking back along the Embankment. Look for **Shell Mex House** ☐ to your right —

it has the largest clock in London. You will also see the **Victoria Embankment Gardens** ☐ and, next to the river, **Cleopatra's Needle** ☐. It dates from 1500 BC and weighs 180 tons. After a while, you are back where you began. ■

Somerset House

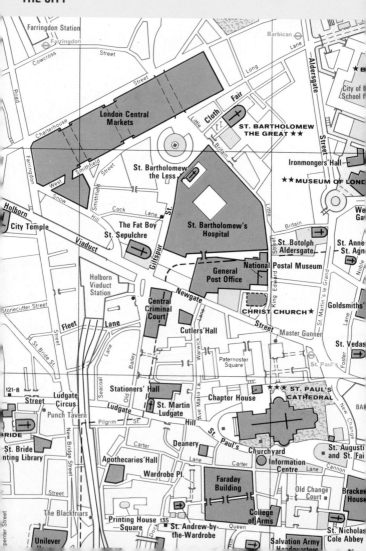

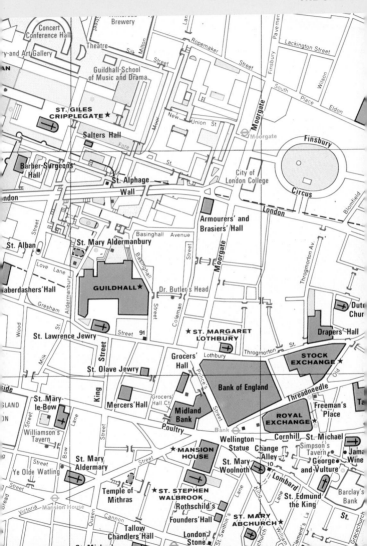

Concert
Conference Hall

Brewery

Theatre

y-and Art Gallery

Silk

Milton

Street

Ropemaker

Street

Lackington Street

Pavement

Finsbury

Wilson

AN

Guildhall School
of Music and Drama

ST. GILES
CRIPPLEGATE ★

New

Union St

Moorgate

Street

Place

Eldon

Salters Hall

Moor

Fore

Moorgate

Finsbury

Barber-Surgeons'
Hall

ondon

ST. GILES
CRIPPLEGATE ★

St. Alphage

City of
London College

Circus

Street

Wall

London

Blomfield

St. Alban

Basinghall   Avenue

Armourers' and
Brasiers' Hall

Moorgate

Dute
Chur

ST. GILES

aberdashers' Hall

St. Mary Aldermanbury

Basinghall

Throgmorton Av.

GUILDHALL ★

Dr. Butler's Head

Gresham

Love Lane

Street

Drapers' Hall

Wood

St.

Coleman

Street

St. Lawrence Jewry

Street

91

★ ST. MARGARET
LOTHBURY

Milk

Throgmorton   St.

STOCK
EXCHANGE ★

King

St. Olave Jewry

Grocers'
Hall

Lothbury

Old

ide

GLAND

N

St. Mary-
le-Bow

Street

Mercers' Hall

Grocers'
Hall Ct

Prince's

Bank of England

Threadneedle

Freeman's
Place

Ta

Williamson's
Tavern

Lane

Bow

Midland
Bank

Street

ROYAL
EXCHANGE ★

Cornhill

St. Michael

Poultry

Bank

Simpson's
Tavern

Jama
Wine

St. Mary
Aldermary

Street

★ MANSION
HOUSE

Wellington
Statue

Change
Alley

10

George
and Vulture

bread

Victoria

Mansion House

Ye Olde Watling

Street

St. Mary
Woolnoth

Lombard

St. Edmund
the King

Barclay's
Bank

St.

Temple of
Mithras

Queen

Cannon

★ ST. STEPHEN
WALBROOK

Rothschild's
Founders' Hall

St. Swithin's

Walbrook

ST. MARY
ABCHURCH ★

King

Lane

Clement's   La

Glace

Tallow
Chandlers' Hall

London
Wall

St. Michael

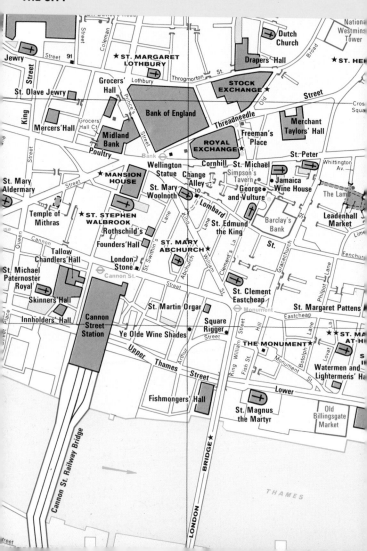

THE CITY

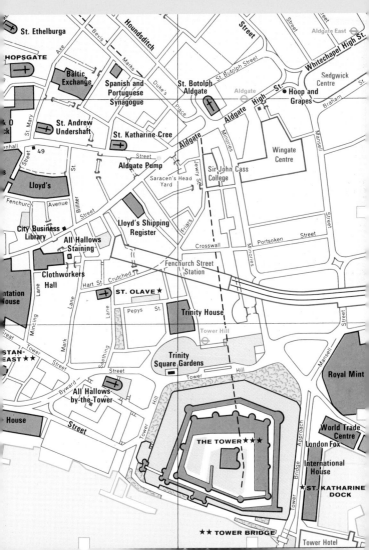

ST PAUL'S/OLD BAILEY

St Paul's Cathedral

● Start at Blackfriars Underground. Down to the right is the **Mermaid Theatre** ☐ in Puddle Dock. Walk along Queen Victoria Street past the **College of Arms** ☐ which, since receiving its charter from Richard III in 1484, has had absolute authority concerning family pedigrees and Coats of Arms. At Peter's Hill, turn left and climb the steps. This is not the usual view of **St Paul's Cathedral** ☐ but it is one of the best, and the one that Sir Christopher Wren had each morning as he was ferried across the river from the house he lived in while building it. There has been a Christian church on this site since at least AD 604. The old cathedral was destroyed in the Great Fire of 1666 which gave Wren his opportunity. Climb up to the **Whispering Gallery** ☐ and look for the monuments to the **Duke of Wellington** ☐, **Lord Nelson** ☐, the English poet **John Donne** (1573-1631) ☐, and, of course, to **Sir Christopher Wren** ☐. His simple tomb has a Latin inscription which means 'Reader, if you seek his monument, look about you'. From the front steps of St Paul's, go down Ludgate Hill (looking back for the more usual view) and turn right into **Old Bailey** ☐. At the end is the **Central Criminal Court** ☐ built on the site of the infamous Newgate Prison. After Tyburn was closed, executions took place in front of Newgate from 1783 until 1867. ➡

The goddess Justice above the Old Bailey (below left); and Smithfield (below)

70

The Bishops Finger   *Whitbread's brewery*

The Barbican

Cross over into Giltspur Street and up to **Smithfield** : London's main meat market and the largest in the world, it has a bloody history. Mary Tudor had 270 Protestants burned here; two centuries earlier Wat Tyler, leader of the Peasants' Revolt, was cut down at Smithfield in front of the King. More cheerful is the curiously named **Bishops Finger** □ pub. A brisk walk down Long Lane brings you to **Aldersgate** □ and the **Barbican** □, the exciting cultural, commercial, and residential complex built around the ancient City Wall. Continue down Beech Street into Chiswell Street to find **Whitbread The Brewery** □, then make your way back through the Barbican complex to the exciting **Museum of London** □ at the corner of Aldersgate and City Wall. Here you can find out more about the fascinating story of London before making your way back down Aldersgate to St Paul's. ∎

The Museum of London

THE CITY

● The only way to explore the heart of the City of London is to start at Bank Underground Station and use the map on page 66 to help you find your own way through the maze of ancient streets and alleyways. If you can, choose a working day because only then is the City alive — and there are people to ask the way if you get lost! Here are some of the things you should try to see but, remember, the City is a working place not a museum, and it is often not possible to enter buildings. If Bank Underground is the centre of a clock, we will start at 3 o'clock. **Cornhill** ☐ was once a grain market. **St Michael's Cornhill** ☐ is built on Saxon foundations. London's first coffee house opened in **St Michael's Alley** ☐ in 1652. In 1840, the composer Mendelssohn played the organ in **St Peter's Cornhill** ☐. **The George and Vulture** ☐ was established in 1600. **Leadenhall Market** ☐ deals in high-quality meat and game and has a fine pub, **The Lamb** ☐. The financier, Edward Lloyd, started to underwrite shipping in a coffee house in 1691. **Lloyds of London** ☐ is now the centre of the world's insurance industry. ➡

Leadenhall Market (above); and Lloyds of London (right)

The Mansion House (right)

Lombard Street ☐ takes its name from the Italian merchants who became money lenders here as early as the thirteenth century. Medieval bankers hung signs in the street, a practice maintained by Barclay's, William and Glyn's, Martins, and Lloyd's. **St Mary Woolnoth** ☐ was built by Wren's most talented pupil, Nicholas Hawksmoor. Wren's **St Edmund the King** ☐ was restored after being bombed in 1917. The London Metal Exchange is in **Plantation House** ☐. **King William Street** ☐ is named after William IV, king of Great Britain and Ireland from 1830 to 1837. Beyond **St Clement's Eastcheap** ☐ is the **Monument** ☐ to the Great Fire of 1666 which began in **Pudding Lane** ☐. This is a fishy area, and before Billingsgate Fish Market was moved in 1982, the smell rose even to the top of the Monument (which is worth the climb).

Fishmongers Hall ☐ houses one of the oldest and richest of the City's livery companies. Preserved within is the dagger with which a guild member, then Lord Mayor, killed Wat Tyler in 1381. **The Mansion House** ☐ is the official residence of the Lord Mayor of London, where the Sword of State, Chain of Office, and Great Mace are kept together with other treasures. Each new Lord Mayor must present himself to the monarch after his installation in November; this is the popular pageant known as The Lord Mayor's Show and paid for by him. Dick Whittington, who was Lord Mayor four times (in 1397, 1398, 1406, and 1419) must have been very wealthy indeed! ➡

The Monument

➡ **St Stephen Walbrook** □ was hit by a bomb during the Blitz of World War 2 but is now restored. **The London Stone** □ is said to be the Roman *milliarium* from which all distances were measured. **The Temple of Mithras** □ was discovered during excavation: the head of the Roman sun god is in the Museum of London. St Mary Aldermary has a sword rest by the famous carver and sculptor Grinling Gibbons (1648-1721), and stained glass commemorating London's courage during the air raids of World War 2 which destroyed so much of the City. **Poultry** □ is, of course, where medieval poulterers plied their trade; it becomes **Cheapside** □ which was once London's greatest market — 'cheap' means to haggle. **Mercer's Hall** □ houses the richest of all the livery companies. Of **St Olave Jewry** □ only the tower remains. This was the Jewish quarter of the City in the Early Middle Ages. **The Guildhall** □ dates from 1411 when the City's great livery companies combined to build it. This is where all the major civic functions take place, including the sumptuous Lord Mayor's Banquet. Princes Street runs between the **Midland Bank** □ and **Grocer's Hall** □ (in the twelfth century they were known as 'pepperers') and the **Bank of England** □, affectionately known as the 'old lady of Threadneedle Street'. In its vaults are the nation's gold reserves and it alone can issue paper money. Look for the Bank of England messengers; they wear pink tail coats and scarlet waistcoats. **St Margaret Lothbury** □ is the last church completed by Sir Christopher Wren except for St Paul's. ➡

The Temple of Mithras (top); The Guildhall (centre); and the Bank of England (bottom)

On the other side of the wonderfully named **Threadneedle Street** ☐ (look out for plaques marking the site of **Lloyd's Coffee House** ☐ and the birthplace of the English theologian and author, **Cardinal Newman** ☐) is the **Royal Exchange** ☐ which now houses the London International Financial Futures Exchange. The **Stock Exchange** ☐ is close by

between Old Street and Throgmorton Street. **The Merchant Taylors' Hall** ☐ is yet another City building, bombed and rebuilt — theirs is the largest guild. **St Helen Bishopsgate** ☐ is a magnificent church known as 'the Westminster Abbey of the City'. **St Ethelburga** ☐ is one of London's oldest churches. Henry Hudson, the English navigator and explorer of the fifteenth and sixteenth centuries, who gave his name to Hudson's Bay, took communion here before sailing off to try to discover the North-west Passage. The **Baltic Exchange** ☐ is for merchants dealing in oil, timber, grain, and other 'floating' cargoes. **St Andrew Undershaft** ☐ takes its name from a famous maypole which was set up in the churchyard every May Day, so tall it overshadowed the church. The **Spanish and Portuguese Synagogue** ☐ is the oldest in England, dating from 1657. ■

The Royal Exchange

The Stock Exchange

● Start at Tower Hill Underground. **Tower Hill** ☐ has seen some of the most terrible events in English history. Look for the square of paving surrounded by chain linking in the garden of **Trinity Square** ☐ to the south of **Trinity House** ☐. This was the site of the scaffold on which at least seventy-five people, who had been held at the Tower, were executed. You will also see **War Memorials** ☐ to the merchant seamen who perished in two world wars, each man's name listed under his ship. The **Tower of London** ☐ itself is a fascinating place which played an important role in English history for more than 900 years, but it has few happy memories. Here Henry VI was murdered while saying his prayers. To this day someone comes each year from the two colleges he founded — Eton and Kings College Cambridge — to lay lilies and roses on the spot. Anne Boleyn was greeted with flowers when she came to the Tower in 1533 for her coronation; only three years later she was executed there. Brighter attractions are the **Crown Jewels** ☐ and the colourful **Beefeaters** ☐, although the Tower's **ravens** ☐ capture the mood better. ➡

Leave the Tower and skirt round the outside up on to **Tower Bridge** ☐. Its two 1000-ton drawbridges have been raised more than half-a-million times since it was completed in 1894. **The Tower Bridge Museum** ☐ on the far side is worth seeing and do not miss the view from the walkways. Recross the bridge to visit **St Katherine's Dock** ☐ down to the right where interesting boats, including original Thames barges, are moored. Returning to the Underground you will see the fine building which once housed the **Royal Mint** ☐. ■

*The Tower of London (opposite);
Tower Bridge (right); and
St Katherine's Dock (below)*

● Start at the East Exit of Aldgate East Underground coming out into **Whitechapel High Street** ☐. On the left, you will see a blue plaque to one of the finest World War 1 poets, **Isaac Rosenberg** ☐. Soon you will come to **Brick Lane** ☐ where Jack the Ripper once stalked. Further on, across the road is the **Whitechapel Bell Foundry** ☐ of Mears and Stainbank who have given voice to London's churches (and many more) since 1570. They cast Big Ben, and recast the famous bells of St Clement's which had not said 'Oranges and Lemons' since they were bombed in 1941. On the same side,

further along you will glimpse the minaret of the **East London Mosque** ☐. The East End has always been a melting pot of different races and cultures: once Huguenots and Jews now Bangladeshis and Bengalis. Recross the road. Walking back past Aldgate East, you will see the **Whitechapel Art Gallery** ☐ and London's most famous Jewish restaurant, **Blooms** ☐. Cross Commercial Street, go past another exit to Aldgate East, and round the corner in Goulston Street you will see **Tubby Isaacs Jellied Eels** ☐ stall. On a Sunday morning, this part of London's East End is at its liveliest, especially **Petticoat Lane Market** ☐ which begins at the bottom of Middlesex Street further along and runs up to Liverpool Street Station. ■

The East London Mosque (left)

● Start at London Bridge Station and make your way by the footbridge down to London Bridge City and the river where you will find **Hay's Galleria** ☐ and **HMS Belfast** ☐. This cruiser had a distinguished war record and opened the 'D'-Day bombardment in 1944. In Tooley Street, you will find the **London Dungeon** ☐ exhibition. Go up Duke's Hill and left down Borough High Street looking out for the pub sign of **The George** ☐. This is the very last galleried inn in London and features in Dickens's *Little Dorrit*. ➡

Hay's Galleria (above); and HMS Belfast *(below)*

The George

Go back towards the bridge and cross over into **Borough Market** ☐, the city's oldest fruit and vegetable market which was held on London Bridge itself until 1756. Nearby is **Southwark Cathedral** ☐, a fine Gothic building that has associations with Shakespeare. The founder of Harvard University was baptized there, and the **Harvard Chapel** ☐ dedicated to him is much visited. When you recross **Borough High Street** ☐ to return to London Bridge Station, remember that this road was London's main artery for hundreds of years. Kings and armies, bishops and pilgrims, and all the important figures in English history passed by here. Until 1749 London Bridge was the only bridge over the river and this was the main highway to Europe. ■

Southwark Cathedral (below); Harvard Chapel (right)

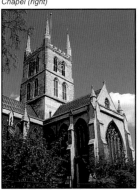

● Start at London Bridge Station. Cross Borough High Street and go down the steps to Southwark Cathedral. From Cathedral Street, you will see the *Kathleen & May* □ moored. Follow Pickford's Wharf round by the river into **Clink Street** □. The old Clink Prison was here, and it gave us the word meaning jail. All that now remains of **Winchester Palace** □ is the Rose Window of the Great Hall. Passing under Cannon Street Railway Bridge you will come to the **Anchor Inn** □ on Bankside with fine views of the City across the river. You are really in Shakespeare territory now.

Look for the site where they are rebuilding the **Globe Theatre** □, perhaps going down **Bear Garden Street** □ to visit **Shakespeare's Globe Museum** □. ➡

The Kathleen & May *(above); and the Rose Window of Winchester Palace (below)*

Continuing along Bankside by the river, you will come to the **Provost's Lodging** ☐ and, next door, the house where **Sir Christopher Wren** ☐ lived while building St Paul's. The riverside walk will eventually take you under Blackfriar's Railway Bridge. Climb the steps up on to Blackfriar's Bridge and cross over to the Underground. On the bridge look for the splendid crest of the **London Chatham and Dover Railway** ☐, and the well-known landmark of the **Oxo Tower** ☐. ∎

The Provost's Lodging (above)

The crest of the London Chatham and Dover Railway (below left); and the Oxo Tower (below)

● Start at Westminster Underground. Turn left and cross Westminster Bridge. To the left you will see **Charing Cross Railway Bridge** ☐; the building on the far side is **County Hall** ☐. Keep left and go down the steps, taking time to admire the **dolphin lamps** ☐. Keep by the river and you will come to the **Jubilee Gardens** ☐ in front of the **Shell Centre** ☐. Go under the railway. Straight ahead is the **Royal Festival Hall** ☐ and beyond that the **National Theatre** ☐. If you explore, you will also find the **National Film Theatre** ☐, **Queen Elizabeth Hall** ☐, **Hayward Gallery** ☐, and the **Museum of the Moving Image** ☐. ➡

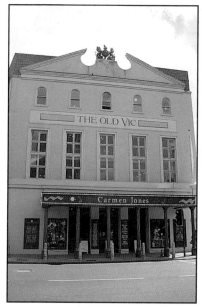

From the South Bank, make your way into Waterloo Road which is a continuation of Waterloo Bridge. Pass under the railway bridge where one of The Great Train Robbers now sells flowers and you will soon see the **Old Vic** ☐, one of London's best-loved theatres. To the right is Lower Marsh, the lively lunchtime market, to the left is **The Cut** ☐. A little way up on the left is a traditional London **Pie and Eel shop** ☐ and, beyond that, the **Young Vic** ☐. Go to the end of The Cut to see a famous boxing pub called **The Ring** ☐ before returning to **Waterloo Station** ☐. ■

The Old Vic theatre (above); a traditional Pie and Eel shop (above right); The Ring (below); and Waterloo Station (below right)

● Start at **Waterloo Station** ☐, pausing to look at the **building for the Channel Tunnel** ☐. Leave the station at the door by Platform 1 and turn right down the ramp. Go left down Leake Street into **Lower Marsh Market** ☐ which is full of bustle at lunchtime. Explore the market, then go back past where you entered and turn left into Westminster Bridge Road; then fork right into Kennington Road for the **Imperial War Museum** ☐ built on the site of Bedlam, the eighteenth-century lunatic asylum. Opposite, in Lambeth Road, is where **Captain Bligh** ☐ of *Mutiny on the Bounty* lived. ➡

The bustle of Lower Marsh Market (above left); and the Imperial War Museum (left)

The lion made for the Lion Brewery (above); Lambeth Palace (opposite)

Further down Kennington Road at **No. 287**  is where Charlie Chaplin lived as a boy. After the Imperial War Museum, cross Kennington Road and continue down Lambeth Road. Have you heard of the song and dance called *The Lambeth Walk*? Lambeth Walk is now rebuilt but the old street, once famous for its market, is on your left. At the end you will come to **Lambeth Palace** ☐, the London home of Archbishops of Canterbury for 800 years —the first was Stephen Langton. Also of interest is the **Museum of Garden History** ☐. Cross over Lambeth Palace Road and go right, following the Albert Embankment along by the river. Go up the steps over Westminster Bridge and down the other side, going right at the Jubilee Gardens for Waterloo. The **lion** ☐ that you pass at the end of Westminster Bridge was made for the Lion Brewery in 1837. ∎

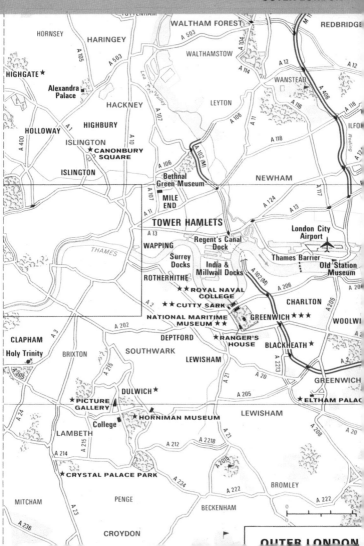

This book is mainly about Central London. But look at the map on the previous pages to see the host of interesting places there are to visit on a day's outing from the centre. You can go by train, underground, or bus or, for some destinations, use London's oldest highway — the River Thames.

River launches will take you to **Kew Gardens** ☐. In the other direction are the **Thames Barrier** ☐ and Greenwich where you can see *Cutty Sark* ☐, last of the sailing clippers, the **Royal Naval College** ☐ and **National Maritime Museum** ☐, and the **Royal Observatory** ☐ on the world's **Zero Meridian of Longitude** ☐. To the north of London are **Hampstead Heath** ☐, once the haunt of highwaymen, and Highgate with its famous **cemetery** ☐ where Karl Marx is buried. To the south is **Hampton Court** ☐, the fabulous palace which Henry VIII took from Thomas Wolsey. **Windsor** ☐ is a wonderful day out. Why not use the train to get there just as Queen Victoria did?

Kew Palace (above); the Cutty Sark *(below left); the Painted Hall, Royal Naval College (below); the Royal Observatory (opposite top left); Hampton Court (opposite top right); and Windsor Castle (opposite)*

INDEX

INDEX

© I-Spy Limited 1995
ISBN (paperback) 1 85671 148 X

Michelin Tyre Public Limited Company
Edward Hyde Building, 38 Clarendon Road,
Watford, Herts WD1 1SX
MICHELIN and the Michelin Man are Registered Trademarks of Michelin

A CIP record for this title is available from the British Library.

Edited and designed by Curtis Garratt Ltd

The Publisher gratefully acknowledges the contribution of Richard Garratt who provided the majority of the photographs in this I-Spy book. Additional photographs by Pitkin Pictorials; cover and title page courtesy of Philip Craven.

London is changing all the time but every care has been taken in the preparation of this I-Spy book to ensure that the factual information was correct at the time of going to press. Neither the publisher nor the editors accept any responsibility whatsoever for any loss, damage, injury, or inconvenience sustained or caused as a result of using this I-Spy book.

Printed in Spain by Graficromo, S.A.